Original title:
Creative Insights

Copyright © 2024 Swan Charm
All rights reserved.

Editor: Jessica Elisabeth Luik
Author: Kätriin Kaldaru
ISBN HARDBACK: 978-9916-86-319-0
ISBN PAPERBACK: 978-9916-86-320-6

Ephemeral Sparks

In the briefest flash, our moments blaze,
A dance of light in fleeting days.
Gone in whispers, silence speaks,
Time's soft hand, so swift it streaks.

Stars ignite, then fade away,
Endless night consumes the day.
Echoes wane, memories part,
In shadows, still, they touch the heart.

Life's a spark, a fleeting crest,
Burning bright, then laid to rest.
Cherish now, for soon it's past,
The fire's glow will never last.

Shadows and Light

In twilight's dance, both dark and bright,
A blend of shadow, blend of light.
Contrast etches, shapes define,
In the balance, worlds entwine.

Day and night, the shifting veil,
Fables told in moonlight pale.
Ebony and ivory weave,
Textures rich, the night to grieve.

Mornings pierce with rays of gold,
What was hidden, then unfolds.
In the stillness, one can find,
Ephemeral, the world aligned.

Wellspring of Wonder

Deep within the mind's embrace,
Springs a fount of endless grace.
Wells of dreams and thoughts untamed,
In this source, the world acclaimed.

Curiosity, the heart's desire,
Ignites the soul, sets thoughts on fire.
Endless pools of questions flow,
From this well, all knowledge grows.

Sip the waters, taste the muse,
Crafting worlds with every use.
In the depths of wonder found,
Imagination's sky unbound.

Twilight of Ideas

As sun descends, thoughts take flight,
In the twilight, sparks ignite.
Ideas bloom in fading glow,
Twilight's breath, their whispers show.

In these hues of dusk's embrace,
Concepts drift in gentle space.
Midnight musings, silent streams,
Glow with fragments of our dreams.

When the day begins to fade,
Wisdom births in night's cascade.
In the quiet's subtle veil,
Ideas bloom, without fail.

Chronicles of Thought

In shadows deep where musings lie,
A whisper of the mind's own sky,
Through corridors of dreams unsought,
Unfurls the chronicles of thought.

By starlit pools, reflections gleam,
In quiet moments, wisdom's theme,
From ancient tales to futures caught,
Unravel the chronicles of thought.

Insight Embers

Within the night, a spark ignites,
Insight embers, burning bright,
With every flicker, shadows dance,
Ideas spiral, take their chance.

Through veils of mist, they find their way,
To morning light from darkest bay,
And as the dawn reveals its glow,
Insight embers start to show.

Mystical Mindscape

A realm where dreams and thoughts entwine,
Mystical mindscape, silent shrine,
With colors born of hidden hues,
And whispers of forgotten clues.

Beyond the veil of common sight,
Through gardens of the starlit night,
A passage framed by ancient lore,
Mystical mindscape to explore.

Waves of Epiphany

Upon the sea of endless thought,
Waves of epiphany are sought,
They crest and fall with rhythmic grace,
In tides of wisdom we embrace.

A moment's calm, a lightning strike,
Revelation's swift, precise-like,
In ocean's vast, the mind sets free,
On waves of epiphany.

Mind's Palette

Brushstrokes of thoughts on consciousness spread,
Colors of dreams in vibrant threads.
Imagination's hues, they blend and merge,
Creating worlds on the psyche's verge.

Conflict and peace, a canvas innate,
Shades of joy with sorrow relate.
Every emotion a vivid streak,
In the gallery of the mystique.

Ideas that shimmer like morning dew,
Pastels of memories, bright and true.
Tranquil blues and feverish reds,
In the recesses where the mind treads.

Reflection in Innovation

Mirrors of progress, reflecting anew,
Concepts reshaped, evolving through.
Shadows of past with future's sheen,
Invention's light crafting unseen.

Thoughts converge in a spark's embrace,
Transforming realms in a silent race.
Each reflection, a vision clear,
In the realm of possibility, no frontier.

Fusion of dreams in reality's gaze,
Innovative paths in uncharted maze.
Reflections shape tomorrow's face,
In the creative spirit's grace.

Seeds of Wonder

Tiny whisper in earth's embrace,
Potential in every sheltered space.
Sprouts of curiosity, tendrils of thought,
From every seed, a tree is wrought.

In fertile ground, the mind does sow,
Dreams take root in the space below.
Nature's wisdom in each small seed,
A universe grows from a single deed.

Wonder's seeds in hearts are sown,
From these small starts, ideas have grown.
Branches reaching, seeking light,
With every dawn, a new height.

Emergent Patterns

From chaos, order takes its flight,
Hidden patterns come to light.
Symphony in nature's dance,
Emergence leads us in a trance.

Leaf and spiral, subtle sign,
Threads of life, in design align.
Fractal forms in endless play,
Cosmic rhythm in night and day.

In randomness, there lies a scheme,
Waves of beauty, endless dream.
Patterns woven, rich and grand,
By nature's hand, in every strand.

Expanding the Horizon

Beyond the mountain, past the skies,
A world unfolds, a new sunrise.
The sun's embrace, the sky's conspire,
In endless blue, dreams aspire.

Horizons stretch, a canvas wide,
With every step, new paths collide.
The wind's whisper, a guiding song,
To realms unknown, we drift along.

Breath of dawn, in twilight's glow,
Nurtures seeds where dreams shall grow.
Boundaries fade, horizons blend,
In infinite loops, our spirits mend.

Whirl of Wonder

In a dance of light, colors swirl,
A mystic spin in nature's whirl.
Leaves of autumn kiss the air,
Wonder lies in moments rare.

Glimmers chase the moon's soft glow,
Stars align in cosmic flow.
Magic breathes in every seam,
Life unfolds in fleeting dream.

Rainbows bridge the skies anew,
Spectrum gaze in morning dew.
In the whirl, hearts pulse faster
Through realms unknown, chasing after.

Uncharted Territories

Maps unrolled, but edges tear,
In unknown seas, we boldly dare.
Compass spins in twilight's hold,
Mystery's tale to be retold.

Voyage through the shadows cast,
Chart the stars, learn from the past.
In the dark, luminescent signs,
Lost and found in cosmic lines.

Journey forth where dreams reside,
In unmarked lands, our spirits bide.
Blur the lines, seek mysteries,
In timeless waves, new histories.

Echoing Depths

Caves of silence, whispers hum,
Songs of earth in hidden strum.
Shadow's veil, a curtain drawn,
Depths reveal in breaking dawn.

Echoes trace through ancient stone,
Secrets kept, to none they've shown.
In the stillness, breath is found,
In boundless depth, we are unbound.

Ocean's call in moonlit night,
Drowning stars in endless flight.
Depths that speak of ages past,
In silent echoes, truths do last.

Spark and Flame

In twilight's gentle, whispering haze,
A spark ignites the velvet blaze,
Dreams awaken, fires proclaim,
Boundless hope in spark and flame.

Lighting midnight, shadows part,
Embers glow within the heart,
Courage blooms where fears exclaim,
Strength ignites in spark and flame.

Under stars, desires climb,
Passions dance in perfect rhyme,
Night surrenders, dawns the name,
Soul reborn in spark and flame.

Innovator's Quest

In realms where dreams are tightly spun,
A vision seen, a race begun,
Paths untrod, the quest is sung,
Innovator's tale, so young.

Ideas weave in silken thread,
Bold imaginations fed,
Uncharted waters lie ahead,
Follow where the mind is led.

Triumphs soar on winds of change,
Boundaries shift and rearrange,
Future's script, ours to engage,
Innovator's quest, a living stage.

Contours of Thought

In silent chambers, whispers play,
Contours of thought, in soft array,
Reflecting shades of night and day,
Ideas bloom and drift away.

Imagination's brushstrokes bare,
Images float upon the air,
Fields of wonder, gardens rare,
Contours of a dreamer's care.

Inward vistas, boundless seas,
Mind's horizon, endless keys,
Infinite the visions tease,
Contours of thought, a mystic breeze.

Fountain of Notions

A wellspring, endless, flowing free,
Fountain of notions, creativity,
Ripples of a boundless sea,
Infinite in you and me.

Cascade of thoughts in vibrant hue,
Every drop a novel view,
Mysteries old, discoveries new,
Fountain of notions, spirit true.

Inspiration's gentle rain,
Drenched in dreams, we lose our pain,
Bathe in ideas, joy sustain,
Fountain of notions, life's refrain.

Prisms of Perception

In light's embrace, the world unfolds,
Each color speaks what time has told.
Through crystal lenses, truth is seen,
A spectrum vast in shades between.

Refractions pulse with whisper's grace,
To paint the sky on nature's face.
Perceptions shift in twilight hues,
Awakening the heart's true clues.

In prisms born of morning dew,
New visions form, a radiant crew.
The eyes of dawn, they seek and know,
The secrets in the afterglow.

Bound by light, both weak and strong,
We find our place where souls belong.
See through prisms, clear as glass,
Unlocked, undaunted, truths amass.

Wisdom's Lattice

Threads of gold in knowledge's weave,
Lessons old, forever cleave.
In lattice formed by ancients' lore,
We tread with grace upon the floor.

Wisdom's whispers, soft yet clear,
Guide us through both far and near.
In every cell, a story etched,
By sages wise, the world is sketched.

Patterns dance in sacred grounds,
Echoes form in silent sounds.
Through lattice fine, our minds engage,
To read the script on wisdom's page.

Interweave with mindful care,
The strands of truth, beyond compare.
In every knot, a secret lies,
To lift the spirit to the skies.

Veil of Thoughts

Behind the veil where silence grows,
Thoughts take flight in hidden flows.
Shadows dance in twilight's call,
As whispers blend and gently fall.

Within the mind, a silent stream,
Carrying dreams made of cream.
Ephemeral, yet deeply felt,
A realm where fleeting moments melt.

Guardians of the unseen land,
Hold secrets in their tender hand.
Veils of thoughts, both light and dark,
Illuminate wisdom's hidden spark.

Through gauzy mists, our visions roam,
In quiet chambers, thoughts find home.
Veil unveiled, we truly see,
The boundless forms our minds can be.

Dreamer's Expedition

In realms where dreams begin to weave,
An endless tale they will conceive.
Across the stars, on winds they glide,
In shadow's cloak and moonlight's tide.

Through caverns deep and mountains high,
Dreamers walk where angels fly.
Horizons bend to match their quest,
Each heartbeat leads with rhythmic zest.

Navigators of a midnight sea,
Charting courses wild and free.
In dreams, they find what life may lack,
Guided by the zodiac.

Every journey lights the night,
With bursts of hope and pure delight.
Dreamers' path, though faint it glows,
A route where endless wonder flows.

Serendipitous Paths

In the whisper of the dawn,
Where shadows softly play,
Paths cross without a plan,
Guiding hearts astray.

Steps taken without thought,
Lead to places unforeseen,
Serendipity's gentle hand,
Crafts moments so serene.

Underneath the starry sky,
Chance meetings bloom and grow,
Connections birthed in mystery,
In twilight's subtle glow.

A journey's unforeseen twists,
Weaves stories interlaced,
Fates entwined by happenstance,
In unexpected grace.

Wander where the unknown calls,
Trust the turns uncharted,
For often in life's winding roads,
New dreams are gently started.

Wonders Unfolded

Amidst the dawn's first light,
A symphony begins,
Nature's wonders wake and bloom,
With choruses like hymns.

The petals of a flower,
Unfurl in morning dew,
A canvas painted fresh each day,
With colors ever-new.

Mountains guard the valleys,
Silent sentinels of old,
Whispering of ages past,
In stories yet untold.

The ocean's rhythmic dance,
To shores both far and near,
Carries secrets on its waves,
For those who dare to hear.

Each moment holds a wonder,
Each breath a mystery,
In the world's vast tapestry,
Lives nature's artistry.

Echoes of Imagination

In the silence of the night,
Dreams begin to weave,
Tales of far-off places,
Of wonders we believe.

Mountains kissed by colored skies,
Rivers that are gold,
In the realm of fantasy,
Stories yet untold.

Whispers of forgotten times,
Echo in our dreams,
Impossible adventures,
On enchanted streams.

Castles in the cotton clouds,
Dragons in the mist,
In our minds they come alive,
By mere thought, exist.

Boundless is the power,
Of imagination's flight,
Bringing to the mundane,
A wondrous ray of light.

A Canvas of Thoughts

Thoughts like strokes of color,
Paint dreams upon the mind,
Each hue a vivid memory,
In patterns intertwined.

Reflections of the inner world,
On a canvas wide,
Blend the light of hopes and fears,
In seamless, shifting tide.

Passions in bold crimson,
Wisdom etched in gray,
Every thought a masterpiece,
Created day by day.

Ideas swirl like tempests,
In a visionary gale,
Crafting realms and stories,
In an endless tale.

In the gallery of moments,
Each frame a captured thought,
Life becomes a masterpiece,
In every dream we've sought.

Luminous Ideas

In the quiet of the night, they gleam,
Ideas flicker like stars unseen,
Through the darkness, they softly beam,
Lighting paths to wonders, serene.

Born of whispers and silent dreams,
Invisible currents, a creative stream,
They twist and turn in moonlit scenes,
Chasing dawn's elusive gleam.

Bright thoughts ignite, and shadows flee,
In the realm where vision is free,
They dance on waves of mystery,
Crafting shapes we yearn to see.

From the mind's depth, soaring high,
Words and images touch the sky,
In the confluence of sight and sigh,
Luminous ideas never die.

Patterns in the Air

Beneath the blue, the clouds convene,
Sketching tales and forms unseen,
They drift and swirl in a vast machine,
Weaving visions in between.

The birds align in silent flight,
Tracing rhythms day and night,
Invisible threads in luminous light,
Patterns in the air ignite.

Leaves that flutter, whispers shared,
In every branch, a secret paired,
The wind breathes life where none dared,
Crafting moments, wholly bared.

From the chaos, order born,
In each sunrise, fresh patterns adorn,
We find connections, forlorn,
In the ethereal, our hearts are drawn.

Uncharted Territory

Set forth upon the unknown seas,
Where dreams are whispering in the breeze,
Horizons call with cryptic keys,
Unlocking realms where time may freeze.

Mountains rise from memories,
Valleys hush with ancient pleas,
Every step, a brand-new tease,
In uncharted territory, we find ease.

Seek the paths that no one knows,
In the wilderness of ebb and flow,
Through the shadows, through the glows,
Every journey, wisdom bestows.

Unknown lands of mind and heart,
To map the new, to chart the start,
In the quest, we play our part,
Uncharted territory—our art.

Beyond the Familiar

Step outside the lines you trace,
In the comfort of known space,
Venture forth, find your pace,
Beyond the familiar, lies grace.

In every turn, a hidden face,
In every corner, a secret place,
The heart's rhythm, a tender chase,
New horizons, we embrace.

What we fear is often kind,
Unknown paths shape the mind,
From the mundane, we unbind,
In the unusual, we find.

Dare to dream, dare to stray,
Through the fog, find your way,
In the unknown, hearts play,
Beyond the familiar, breaks day.

Dawn of Innovation

In shadows night began to flee,
The dawn of dreams took flight.
A spark of brilliance set us free,
To weave with threads of light.

Beyond horizons yet unseen,
Ideas soared on wings.
Innovation danced between,
The tangible things.

Factories rose, machines conceived,
Transforming live's scenes.
With every thought profoundly perceived,
We built our thriving dreams.

Bound by no limits, vision and lore
Crafted wonders anew.
Progress on the constant shore,
Where aspirations grew.

From whispers of the thoughtful mind,
Creation's joy was spun.
In this epoch mankind doth find,
A future brightly won.

Alchemy of Words

In cauldrons of a poet's craft,
Emotions blend and churn.
Alchemy of words, in lines draft,
Multi-hued passions burn.

With prose that dances, takes a flight,
Converting thoughts to gold.
Each phrase a gem in moonlit night,
Mantras of old retold.

Through alchemy our hearts engage,
In metaphors and rhymes.
Transmuting scenes upon a page,
Transcending realms of time.

From ink and quill, flows alchemist,
With eloquence so fine.
In words of sages, lovers kissed,
In verses intertwine.

Thus poets blend with subtle art,
The essence of their soul.
In every stanza they impart,
Elixirs that console.

Evolving Dimensions

In spaces vast our dreams disperse,
Evolving as they please.
Dimensions shift in playful verse,
Amongst the cosmic seas.

A multiverse of forms we find,
Where thoughts can freely roam.
In endless loops the mind's entwined,
Within its boundless home.

Through timelines we, relentless, spin,
Colliding with our fate.
Realities we oft' begin,
New worlds we animate.

An abstract dance of life and space,
Fluidly transcend.
In every step we leave a trace,
Patterns that never end.

Each evolving shift we embrace,
The mysteries profound.
In every sphere, time's tender grace,
Infinity unbound.

Mystic Vignettes

In twilight's gentle, quiet veil,
A sight of mystic lore.
Secrets whispered, moonbeams pale,
Vignettes from days of yore.

In shadows deep the faeries dance,
Their laughter soft and pure.
A world within a fleeting glance,
Magic we once knew for sure.

Within the mist old temples stand,
Relics of wisdom's reign.
Each silent stone, a mystic hand,
A map to arcane gain.

Enchanted forests weave their tales,
As breezes softly sigh.
Amongst the glades where silence hails,
The muses gently lie.

Through vignettes we wander free,
In mystic realms that glow.
An ancient song, a timeless plea,
In dreams our spirits grow.

Serendipity's Edge

Upon the cusp of chance we stand,
Where fate and fortune intertwine.
Unexpected currents guide our hand,
To paths unknown, where stars align.

A whisper in the autumn breeze,
A subtle hint of what may come.
In serendipity, we seize,
The fleeting moment, fully numb.

The edge of mystery we tread,
With hearts alight and eyes wide.
In twilight's glow, softly led,
Beyond the realms of time we glide.

Tales unwritten, futures bright,
In serendipity's gentle hold.
Through shadowed days and moonlit nights,
Our destiny's tale foretold.

Inventive Echoes

In caverns of the mind, we trace,
Ideas born in silent space.
From voids of thought, they form and race,
To realms where dreams and truths embrace.

With every beat and whispered word,
Inventive echoes rise and fall.
The silent voices, still unheard,
They paint the skies and break the wall.

Through haze and mist, the visions flit,
Like fireflies in summer's night.
By passion's spark, we're gently lit,
In twilight's glow, our minds take flight.

Crafting worlds from shadows bright,
A tapestry of sound and hue.
In inventive echoes, purest light,
And endless skies of midnight blue.

The Spark Within

Deep within the soul's vast sea,
Lies a spark, forever bright.
Invisible yet wild and free,
Guiding us through darkest night.

In moments still, it flickers on,
A beacon to the truth inside.
Through trials faced and hopes forgone,
In our hearts, it will abide.

A fire that neither dims nor fades,
A constant in the storm of time.
Through all of life's uncertain grades,
This spark within, our silent chime.

In joy and sorrow, pain and glee,
The spark within will light the way.
A guiding force eternally,
Through night and into each new day.

Streams of Fantasy

In streams of fantasy, we drift,
To realms unknown by waking mind.
In gossamer threads, our dreams we lift,
A tapestry by fate designed.

Through forests deep and skies of gold,
Our spirits soar on wings of light.
In tales of wonder, truth be told,
The boundaries melt in moonlit night.

With every wave that softly breaks,
A new adventure's gently spun.
In streams of fantasy, heart wakes,
And dances with the setting sun.

In dreams, we find what words can't say,
A hidden world, both vast and grand.
Through streams of fantasy, we stray,
To grasp the magic close at hand.

Perception's Grace

A whisper in the silent night,
Flaming stars in heaven's face,
Caught within our fleeting sight,
Bound to time's eternal chase.

Colors blend in seamless flow,
Patterns vast, yet intricate,
Life's complex tapestry does show,
In each thread, a tale to state.

Moments pass like falling leaves,
Each absorbed in nature's fold,
Through the web that life perceives,
Stories new and tales of old.

Eyes perceive what hearts may miss,
In the subtlety of the glance,
A world unfolds in fleeting bliss,
Written in a sacred dance.

Perception's grace, a gift to hold,
In every beat, in every breath,
Through this vision, lives unfold,
Bearing witness, life to death.

Synaptic Symphony

Electric whispers, passing through,
In the night, a spark will fly,
Connections deep, both old and new,
In the brain's vast, endless sky.

Neurons dance in complex beat,
Silent symphonies arise,
Thoughts emerge in pure retreat,
Songs of truth and lullabies.

Messages in coded form,
Traverse landscapes of the mind,
In their pathways, warmth or storm,
Subtle gestures intertwined.

Memory and thought entwine,
Building bridges near and far,
In the dance, unique designs,
Craft the mind's brilliant star.

Synaptic symphony, live on,
In your rhythm, chaos tame,
Life's rich essence gently drawn,
Within the mind's eternal frame.

The Alchemy of Thought

Through the cauldron of the mind,
Elements of dreams conflate,
Ideas in the ether find,
Substance in a crafted state.

Wisdom forged in quiet fires,
Blends the ancient with the new,
In the crucible of desires,
Thoughts take shape in varied hues.

Transformations subtle, bold,
Mingle in the mind's embrace,
Gold from lead, as tales unfold,
Crafting visions, time and space.

Inspiration, fleeting kiss,
Gives to thoughts their golden wings,
By this gentle alchemist,
Change and revelation springs.

The alchemy of thought, profound,
Turns the mundane into art,
In this magic, truth is found,
Science, dreams, and human heart.

Insightful Horizons

In the expanse of knowing's reach,
Past the edge where reason lies,
Horizons brightening, beseech,
A fuller truth to recognize.

Distant dreams in color's glow,
Map the paths of future's gaze,
In each step, we come to know,
Threads of wonder, woven maze.

Insight pierces through the veil,
Light upon the darkened scene,
Revelations softly sail,
In the spaces in between.

Questions lead us further on,
Journey of the open mind,
Toward the rising of the dawn,
Greater vistas, there to find.

Insightful horizons gleam,
Offering their boundless light,
In each heart and every dream,
Whispers of an endless night.

Thoughtscape Horizons

Where the mind's eye wanders free,
Across horizons yet unseen.
Thoughts drift on an endless sea,
In realms where dreams convene.

Mountains rise in shadowed peaks,
Whispers old as time, they speak.
Stars align above, mystique,
Charting paths our hearts do seek.

Oceans vast and skies so wide,
In the thoughtscape we confide.
Mystic winds our minds do ride,
Journeys where our souls reside.

Ever turning, bright and fair,
Ideas blossom in the air.
Visions bloom beyond compare,
In horizons rare, they flare.

As the twilight casts its spell,
Boundaries of thought dispel.
In these realms we learn to dwell,
Where the quiet dreams do swell.

Imaginary Voyages

Set sail on oceans made of dreams,
Where fantasy and wonder streams.
Galleons of hope, it seems,
Are lost in silver moonlight beams.

Islands float on clouds of song,
Skies where magic birds belong.
Traveler's heart beats strong and long,
In lands where wishes can't be wrong.

Rivers whisper tales of old,
Hidden treasures, stories told.
Shores of brilliance to behold,
In realms where courage turns to gold.

Through the stars our ships will glide,
On the cosmic winds we'll ride.
Galaxies in soft moon-tide,
Mark the voyage far and wide.

Every port a mystery,
Unlocked by curiosity.
Journeying through the fantasy,
Imaginary voyages, wild and free.

Layers of Perception

Peel the layers one by one,
Reveal the secrets under sun.
Each new truth a battle won,
In the mind's quiet run.

Shades of thoughts in hues of gray,
Shapes that shift and waltz away.
Through the fog, we find our way,
To see the world in fresh array.

Depths unknown beneath the guise,
Hidden truths in soft disguise.
Through perception's sharpened eyes,
The layers fall and new arise.

Mirrors show us multiple,
Infinite and subtle pull.
Reality so sculptural,
In layers, full and colorful.

As each layer fades to dawn,
All illusions overdrawn.
New perceptions brightly spawn,
In the light of truth, reborn.

Quantum Thoughts

Particles of thought collide,
In the mind where wonders hide.
Quantum leaps from side to side,
Through the cosmos, our thoughts glide.

Waves of wisdom undulate,
In the void, they propagate.
Ideas' light will resonate,
In quantum dreams, we navigate.

Schrödinger's cat in mental maze,
Thoughts exist in endless phase.
Many paths our minds can trace,
In the quantum's boundless space.

Entangled minds, a silent dance,
In the quantum realm's expanse.
Every choice a bright expanse,
Thoughts in superposed romance.

Moments split in micro time,
Infinite, they brightly chime.
In the quantum thought sublime,
We explore the grand design.

Catalyst of Change

In whispers, life does softly weave,
Moments shifting, hearts believe,
A spark ignites in shadows dim,
Transforming all from deep within.

Chaos dances, breaks our chains,
Fires burn through old refrains,
In the ashes, dreams take flight,
Darkness bows to newfound light.

Winds of time, with gentle kiss,
Sweep away the night's abyss,
Rebirth springs from every tear,
Bravery conquers silent fear.

Through the storm, the dawn arrives,
Hope ignites and love survives,
The world sways on fate's design,
Change emerges, bright, divine.

Whispered truths, the soul does glean,
From life's canvas, vast and keen,
Each moment, a brushstroke's range,
In our core, the catalyst of change.

Boundless Flow

Rivers carve through ancient stone,
Songs unwritten, yet well-known,
Currents whisper secrets low,
In their dance, life's boundless flow.

Mountains bow to shifting sands,
Time slips through unknowing hands,
Oceans swell in lunar beam,
Tides uplift the sailor's dream.

Stars reflect on silver tides,
Echoes where the heart resides,
Limitless, the sky above,
Boundless, like enduring love.

Sky and sea, a marriage old,
Stories in their depths unfold,
Endless, vast, forevermore,
Nature's breath, the endless shore.

From the brook's soft melody,
To the roar of wild, free sea,
Life within the ebb and flow,
Boundless, where the spirits go.

Inner Alchemy

Echoes in the silent mind,
Treasures hidden, yet to find,
Whispers from the soul's deep sea,
Transforming through inner alchemy.

Shadows dance in moonlit haze,
Guiding through life's winding maze,
Inward journeys conquer doubt,
Wisdom's seeds within sprout.

Metals turn to purest gold,
Through the fires, truths unfold,
Chaos bends to calm, serene,
Mysteries shed light unseen.

Boundless realms within us wait,
Unlocking paths, altering fate,
In the heart's crucible, free,
Magic of this alchemy.

In reflection's quiet glow,
Scars and blessings subtly show,
Altering course endlessly,
Masterpiece of inner alchemy.

Illuminated Paths

Stars that pierce the velvet night,
Guide lost souls to morning light,
On horizons, hopes rekindle,
Paths illuminated, dreams enkindle.

Lanterns held in trembling hand,
Mark the trails on foreign land,
Shadows wane as courage grows,
In each step, the spirit glows.

Journeys marked by moon's embrace,
Every turn, a sacred grace,
Following where hearts do yearn,
To the knowledge, we return.

Through the darkness, wisdom shines,
Forging links in life's designs,
Every soul, a torch does bear,
Illuminated paths declare.

Life's adventures old and new,
Guided by the twilight hue,
In the glow of truth's soft bath,
We walk the illuminated path.

A Realm of Notions

In the silence of the night,
Where thoughts begin to roam,
Ideas take their flight,
And find a quiet home.

Dreams build a vast domain,
Unseen but crystal clear,
Where fantasies disdain,
The bounds of doubt and fear.

Imaginary seas,
With waves of pure delight,
Carry endless pleas,
From dawn until twilight.

Stars of wisdom gleam,
In this mental space,
Guiding every dream,
Through time and through grace.

Here the mind is free,
To wander as it will,
Crafting what could be,
As it rests, serene and still.

Flights of Fancy

Upon a whim we soar,
Through skies of sapphire hue,
Imagination's door,
Opens wide anew.

Lands of lush green trees,
Rivers swift and clear,
Whisper to the breeze,
Stories we hold dear.

Clouds like cotton float,
In patterns soft and grand,
Each a secret note,
From a distant land.

Birds with wings of gold,
Glide through ether bright,
And mysteries unfold,
In the endless light.

Majesty on high,
Bids the heart to fly,
Where dreams and hopes lie,
Beneath a boundless sky.

The Muse's Whisper

In the quiet of the eve,
When shadows start to sway,
Muses gently weave,
Words within the fray.

Soft as whispers fall,
In the mind's embrace,
They heed the silent call,
Of inspiration's grace.

Ideas intertwine,
Like threads of fine silk,
Crafting every line,
With artistry and skill.

Visions subtly speak,
In hues both bright and dim,
Guiding thoughts that seek,
The echo of a hymn.

With each whispered word,
A world is brought to light,
In the silence heard,
Creation takes its flight.

Revelations in Color

Hues of dawn arise,
In gradients of gold,
Painting morning skies,
With stories yet untold.

Emerald fields awake,
To sunlight's warm caress,
Revelations make,
The heart's unrest confess.

Blues of ocean deep,
Whisper secret tales,
Where mysteries sleep,
And solitude prevails.

Crimson dusk descends,
In splendor rich and bold,
As day's chapter ends,
New visions unfold.

Colors speak in hues,
Of life and love and light,
Bringing forth new views,
In the canvas of the night.

Ethereal Blueprints

In dreams, the stars align above,
Celestial whispers, endless love.
Blueprints light the evening sky,
Where destinies forever lie.

Silken threads of fate entwine,
Designs of life, by hands divine.
Ephemeral, yet so clear,
Guiding us through hope and fear.

Upon this canvas of the night,
Infinite plans come into sight.
Sketches of tomorrow's day,
Patterns in the Milky Way.

Heaven drafts our secret schemes,
Sewn together with moonbeams.
In this ether, pure and true,
We find our paths, like morning dew.

Each constellation, a tale to tell,
Crafted where the spirits dwell.
We navigate through nebulae,
Charting courses in the fray.

Fragments of Brilliance

Glimmers of a shattered mind,
Pieces in the dark we find.
Splinters of a radiant glow,
Painting scenes no words can show.

In reflections of the past,
Echoes of a light so vast.
Mosaic of moments bright,
Basking in their fractured light.

Glistening shards on time's shore,
Gleams that we cannot ignore.
Held within a prism's grasp,
Timeless wonders we unclasp.

Brightness breaks through twilight's veil,
Stories in each fragment tell.
Silent yet profoundly deep,
Brilliant dreams within us keep.

Gathered fragments, pure and true,
Craft a vision, wholly new.
From these pieces, we compose,
A masterpiece, no one knows.

Visionary Pathways

Through the mist, where dreams reside,
Paths unseen, but side by side.
Visionary tracks unfold,
Leading hearts both brave and bold.

Steps we take on trails unseen,
Pursuing what our souls have gleaned.
Illuminated by foresight,
Guided through the darkest night.

Away from shadows of the past,
Onto roads that ever last.
Each footfall, a future prize,
Seen through ever-watchful eyes.

Trails of stardust, silver lines,
Woven through the sands of time.
Journey to a land unknown,
Where all our visions have grown.

Endless pathways to explore,
Opening an unseen door.
With each stride, our spirits rise,
Walking towards untold skies.

Conceptual Tapestry

Threads of thought in hues so bright,
Woven through the endless night.
Patterns form in mind's expanse,
Dances in a silent trance.

Each idea, a colored strand,
Interlaced by wisdom's hand.
Fabric of our deepest dreams,
Crafted from life's flowing streams.

Woven tight with hopes and fears,
Stitched with laughter, sown with tears.
Inspiration's gentle needle,
Shapes the cloth, ever lethal.

Tapestry of great design,
Stories told in every line.
Concepts merging, full and grand,
In a web by vision spanned.

Masterpiece of human thought,
With each thread, creation brought.
Hanging in the gallery,
Of our shared reality.

Sacred Whispers

In the heart of night so deep,
Sacred whispers softly creep.
Moonlight's kiss on earth's embrace,
Healing wounds within their grace.

Stars align in cosmic dance,
Every twinkle fuels your chance.
Mountains hum a quiet tune,
Secrets hidden past the dune.

Listen close, the world's alive,
In the shadows, spirits thrive.
Nature's hymn, a lullaby,
Lift your soul towards the sky.

Ancient echoes, wise and old,
Stories whispered, dreams retold.
In the silence, find your key,
To unlock your destiny.

Feel the whispers in your veins,
Mystic truths that life explains.
In the stillness, worlds collide,
Sacred whispers, be your guide.

Pulse of Epiphany

Threads of thought begin to weave,
Infinite patterns we perceive.
Mind's horizons stretch and bend,
In each moment, worlds transcend.

Lightning strikes of sudden awe,
By the light, we're left in awe.
In the midst of chaos, learn,
Through the fire, a soul will burn.

Chasing sparks in darkest night,
Guiding hands in realms of light.
Boundless visions start to bloom,
Born within, like fragrant plumes.

Whispers of the great unknown,
Seeds of wisdom have been sown.
Through the pulse of epiphany,
Truth reveals its symphony.

Every heartbeat fuels the quest,
In our minds, we find the rest.
From within, the answers gleam,
Pulse of life, our waking dream.

Embers of Thought

Beneath the stars, thoughts ignite,
Embers glowing in the night.
Memories of days gone by,
In the flames, they never die.

Dreams like ashes, drift away,
Leaving scars from yesterday.
Kindle hopes and fan the fire,
Sparks of passion rising higher.

In the depth of midnight's hue,
Find the truth that guides you through.
Flickers of a thousand tales,
In the embers, wisdom hails.

Let the warmth of thought embrace,
In each ember, find your place.
Glimmers of a brighter dawn,
In the shadows, wisdom drawn.

Feeding flames of endless dreams,
Where the heart of life redeems.
Through the embers of the mind,
Peace and purpose you will find.

Visions Unfurled

Upon the edge of dawn's first light,
Visions unfurl, pure and bright.
Every hue, a tale retold,
Mysteries in colors bold.

Through the veil of morning mist,
Whispers of the future kissed.
Painted skies with dreams uncurled,
Secrets of an unseen world.

In each shadow, visions play,
Dancing on the edge of day.
Winds of fate begin to swirl,
On the breeze, dreams unfurled.

Eyes wide open, heart in tune,
Seeking truths beneath the moon.
From the darkness, visions rise,
Bound by stars in cosmic ties.

In the quiet, find the key,
To the realms of destiny.
Every vision, every turn,
In their glow, let passion burn.

Invisible Weave

In the fabric of the air, unknown,
Whispers woven, threads are sown,
Silent patterns, softly drawn,
In a world at breaking dawn.

Silent seams in shadows hide,
Waves that ripple, side by side,
Invisible weaves the night,
Holding dreams in tender plight.

Starlight stitches, gentle beams,
Sew the edges of our dreams,
Moonlight's silver, subtly shown,
In the quiet weave, we've grown.

Cosmic threads in quiet dance,
Binding fate with quiet trance,
Weave the whispers of the night,
In the web of hidden light.

From the loom of cosmic grace,
An unseen hand begins to trace,
Strings of life, both firm and frail,
In the weave, we tell our tale.

Thread of Invention

From the sparks of vivid mind,
Threads of thought in webs aligned,
Invention's call, sharp and bright,
Igniting shadows, birthing light.

Fingers weave the unseen thread,
Ideas forming, living, dead,
In each twist, a world is born,
In the mind, invention sworn.

Gears and cogs of thought collide,
In the heart where dreams reside,
Machinations subtly spin,
Threaded pathways deep within.

Through the loom of sheer delight,
Crafting marvels in the night,
In the crucible of dreams,
Nothing's ever as it seems.

So we stitch the future's form,
Where imagination storms,
In the thread of pure invention,
Lies our boundless, bright intention.

Whimsy's Dance

In the fields where laughter's free,
Whimsy dances, wild with glee,
Skipping, twirling, in the air,
Joyful steps without a care.

Gossamer wings on breezes ride,
In a dance, the world confides,
Playful whispers, sprightly tune,
Dancing 'neath the sun and moon.

Footsteps light on petals soft,
Weaving through the bower oft,
Where the blooms in colors bright,
Join in Whimsy's sweet delight.

In each turn, a story spins,
Wondrous tales on playful winds,
Hear the laughter, feel the trance,
Join in Whimsy's endless dance.

With a heart so pure and light,
Dance away the world's blight,
In the realm where dreams enhance,
Find your joy in Whimsy's dance.

Essence of Enlightenment

In the quiet of the mind,
Essence pure, a treasure find,
Light of wisdom, softly glows,
In the heart where knowledge grows.

Gentle rays of insight gleam,
Through life's ever-flowing stream,
In each whisper, lesson learned,
In the soul, the light, it's burned.

Understanding, softly spread,
Through the threads of words unsaid,
In the silence, wisdom's song,
Guides the spirit, deep and strong.

With each breath, enlightenment,
Essence pure and heaven-sent,
In the depths, a boundless sight,
Guiding through eternal night.

In the stillness, find your peace,
From the grasp of thought, release,
In the essence of the light,
Find the truth in purest sight.

Through the Veil

Across the night a whisper flows,
A silver thread that softly glows,
Through mysteries of ancient tales,
We wander gently through the veils.

The stars above in silence speak,
With secrets only moonlight seeks,
In shadows where the echoes dwell,
We dance within the night's deep swell.

Beneath the dark, the answers hide,
In realms where dreams and truth collide,
With every step a story trails,
As we transcend through hidden veils.

In twilight's arms, the soul rebounds,
Embracing all the lost and found,
In hollowed halls where silence hails,
We breathe and live through timeless veils.

Eternal winds of cosmic lore,
We venture forth, to seek, explore,
In whispers soft, our journey sails,
Forever through the mystic veils.

Universe in a Grain

In single grain a cosmos lies,
A world within where wonders rise,
Infinity in finite form,
The endless dances of a storm.

Each speck of dust, a hidden seas,
With galaxies born on a breeze,
In microcosms spun so tight,
Mirrors reflecting endless light.

Through grains of sand and drops of dew,
The universe reveals its hue,
In every part a whole is seen,
In smallest realms, a boundless dream.

In moments brief, eternity,
The smallest parts all vast and free,
A universe within our hand,
Endless as the shifting sand.

The grains of time in silence pass,
Through endless night, through shimmering glass,
The universe within remains,
A cosmos in each tiny grain.

Cosmic Ripples

In starlit pools, the cosmos wakes,
With every wave a ripple makes,
Through silent space the currents run,
In echoes of the distant sun.

The universe in ripples speaks,
With whispers soft that cosmic seeks,
Each trembling thread a tale untold,
Of mysteries that stars behold.

Through ether's calm, the ripples flow,
In waves of light the secrets show,
A dance of time, a celestial sway,
Through night's embrace, the ripples play.

From quasar's heart to comet's tail,
The ripples sing, the truths unveil,
In every pulse, a burst of light,
Across the dark, through endless night.

In cosmic waves, our fates entwine,
With every ripple, patterns shine,
Through vast expanse, the ripples creak,
The whispers of the stars we seek.

Soul's Alchemy

Within the forge where dreams are cast,
Through trials of fire the heart's recast,
Transmuting lead to gold's embrace,
The alchemy of soul takes place.

Through shadows deep and suffering's reign,
Emerges light from purest pain,
With every tear a gem refined,
In crucibles where fate's designed.

The spirit finds its truest form,
Through tempests wild and quiet storms,
Ascending through the flames of life,
Beyond the realm of mortal strife.

In alchemist's embrace we turn,
To find within, the lessons burn,
The soul's rebirth from earthly clay,
To realms of light, it finds its way.

The magic in the trials we see,
Is soul's profound alchemy,
In fire and grace, the spirit grows,
Through endless night, in golden glows.

Enigmatic Echoes

In shadows deep where silence lies,
Mysterious whispers softly slide.
Between each thought the echo hides,
A dance of minds, a secret guide.

By moonlit glow, the night reveals,
The voices lost, the time it steals.
An ancient song, a heart it heals,
Of dreams, of hopes that night conceals.

A hidden path by fate designed,
The echoes of our souls entwined.
Through veils of mist, the truth we'll find,
The whispered words, the bards remind.

In mirrored streams where questions flow,
The echoes' call, the search to know.
In labyrinths of thought they show,
The mysteries deep, the silent woe.

With each new dawn, the echoes fade,
The shadows cast, a soft parade.
Yet in our hearts, their mark is laid,
The enigmatic dreams they've made.

The Art of Unseen

In silence born, the strokes align,
A painter's hand, a sacred sign.
Invisible the scenes define,
A world rewoven in design.

Through colors lost, the light reveals,
The hidden truths, the heart that feels.
Each brush a whisper, softly heals,
The silent storms the mind conceals.

With unseen hands, the canvas shapes,
The shadowed forms, the light that drapes.
In every hue, a trace escapes,
Of dreams unknown, their silent tapes.

A dance of shades, of love, of strife,
The essence caught in scenes of life.
The unseen art with meaning rife,
It carves the soul like sculptor's knife.

In quiet halls where whispers blend,
The art unseen, the hearts transcend.
For in each stroke, the dreams defend,
A silent tale we comprehend.

Mind's Odyssey

In realms of thought where shadows dwell,
A journey starts, an inner swell.
Through corridors where echoes tell,
Of secrets kept, of dreams that fell.

The mind's own sea, a tempest vast,
On waves of time, the shadows cast.
With sails of hope, the die is cast,
To distant shores of knowledge past.

In twilight's heart, the path unveiled,
Through labyrinths where hope prevailed.
A guide, a spark, the light regaled,
By whispers of the stars entailed.

Among the stars, the quest divides,
Through comet trails and cosmic tides.
The odyssey where truth abides,
In constellations, mind confides.

With every step, the journey's lore,
A tapestry of thought and more.
The odyssey to wisdom's door,
The mind's own quest forevermore.

Beyond Boundaries

In realms unmarked by lines of plight,
Where freedom calls, beyond the sight.
The boundaries fade in endless night,
A flight of souls, a boundless flight.

Through skies uncharted, dreams dictating,
Horizons bright, the heart elating.
The journey wild, exhilarating,
In boundless realms, time activating.

No chains to bind, no walls confine,
The spirit's quest, the heart's design.
In open fields where stars align,
A boundless dance of souls enshrined.

With wings of hope, the limits break,
To worlds unseen, the minds awake.
A cosmic dance, the paths we'll take,
In boundless love, our hearts partake.

Beyond the fields of right and wrong,
The souls unite in endless song.
In freedom's flight where dreams belong,
The boundaries fade, our spirits strong.

Fantasia Realms

Beneath the moon's soft silver glow,
In realms where only dreamers go,
A castle floats on clouds afar,
Whispering tales where wishes are.

Fairies dance in glades unseen,
Weaving magic through the green,
Fantasies breathe in twilight's hush,
Transforming night with gentle blush.

Waves of wonder crest and break,
Mystic creatures come awake,
Night's tapestry, a woven dream,
In Fantasia's realms, all things gleam.

Stars become a guiding light,
Through the realms of endless night,
Unseen landscapes, boundless sky,
Where imagination learns to fly.

In Fantasia's realms, we find,
A place unhinged from mortal mind,
Every tale and myth unfolds,
In this land, where magic holds.

Eureka Moments

In quiet sparks of midnight thought,
Epiphanies, so dearly sought,
Light bulbs flashing, minds ignite,
Revealing truths within the night.

A sudden gleam, a lightning strike,
Ideas bloom with passion's spike,
Eureka moments, clear and bright,
Guide us through the darkest plight.

Whispers of the muse inspire,
Kindling the heart with inner fire,
From chaos, clarity is born,
With every dawn, new hopes adorn.

The journey of the restless mind,
In serendipity confined,
Across the canvas of the soul,
Eureka moments make us whole.

Ephemeral but deeply known,
A flash of brilliance brightly shown,
In these fleeting seconds shine,
The seeds of greatness so divine.

Illusory Lines

Between the real and what is not,
Wander on this tangled plot,
Shadows dance on edge of sight,
Illusory lines in endless night.

Mirrors hold a world so strange,
Reflections shift, perceptions change,
Distorted shapes of what could be,
Lines of truth and fantasy.

Dreams and reality entwine,
Blurred boundaries, a fluid line,
Whispers of another place,
In every mirrored face we trace.

Through the veil of mist and haze,
Navigate the soft-lit maze,
Illusory lines lead the way,
To where imagination's roots lay.

In these realms where limits break,
Paths of wonder we will take,
Lost within the fleeting signs,
In the land of illusory lines.

Sculpting Air

With hands that crave to mold and shape,
Crafting dreams in boundless scape,
Invisible, the silent clay,
Sculpting air at break of day.

Whispers held in tender grasp,
Ephemeral, elusive clasp,
Artistry in strokes unseen,
Breathing life in air serene.

Ideas form in fragile space,
Carving out a timeless grace,
In the stillness, structures rise,
Built from whispers, hopes, and sighs.

A dance of fingers, deft and fair,
Invisible threads woven there,
Every breath, a fleeting form,
Sculpting air that feels so warm.

Creation from shadows spun,
Crafted till the work is done,
In the silence, unaware,
Masterpieces sculpted air.

Soulful Strokes

Upon the canvas, life's hues blend,
In shadows deep and daylight's end,
Brushstrokes whisper tales untold,
In colors warm, in colors cold.

Each layer speaks of joy and pain,
Of love rekindled and fleeting rain,
A masterpiece of heart and mind,
In every stroke, a soul confined.

The artist's hand, both swift and slow,
Crafting worlds where dreams may go,
Canvas whispers dreams anew,
Soulful strokes in every hue.

Through vibrant hues and muted tones,
Eternity within it adjoins,
Depths of passion, heights of flight,
In painted truth, all sorrows, light.

The final flourish, the quiet sigh,
An echo of the spirit's cry,
In soulful strokes, our lives are cast,
Timeless moments, forever grasped.

Infinite Spirit

Beneath the stars, the heart does dream,
Of endless skies and uncharted streams,
In every breath, the cosmos' song,
An infinite spirit, wild and strong.

Through time's vast sea, the soul does glide,
A traveler upon the cosmic tide,
Each moment seized, each heartbeat felt,
In infinite grace, our spirits melt.

The universe whispers secrets old,
In stories vast and legends bold,
We dance within its boundless light,
An infinite spirit, pure and bright.

Galaxies spin in cosmic dance,
A symphony of chance and trance,
In the vast expanse, we find our place,
Infinite spirit in boundless space.

In every heart, the universe thrills,
With hopes and dreams and silent wills,
An endless journey where we meet,
Infinite spirit, ever sweet.

Visceral Notions

Within the marrow, emotions churn,
With visceral fire, senses burn,
A storm of feeling, raw and deep,
In every breath, in every leap.

Passion courses through our veins,
With joy, with sorrow, life's refrains,
Each heartbeat, a thunderous roar,
Visceral notions, to the core.

In whispered words and silent cries,
In gazing eyes and soft goodbyes,
The raw and real come into play,
Visceral notions, night and day.

Flesh and bone, and soul combined,
The depth of feeling intertwined,
Eternal quest for love and truth,
Visceral notions, old and youth.

In every touch, the universe speaks,
In moments strong and moments weak,
An echo of the primal call,
Visceral notions within us all.

The Heart's Concept

Within the chambers, silent beat,
The heart's concept, pure and sweet,
A rhythm flowing, constant, true,
In shades of red, in every hue.

Through valleys deep and peaks so high,
It conquers fear, it reaches sky,
A compass guiding through the storm,
The heart's concept, tender, warm.

In whispered love and fervent plea,
The heart's concept, wild and free,
It binds us close in joy and pain,
In every loss, in every gain.

A vessel of immortal dreams,
Of silver threads and golden seams,
It carries forth through night and day,
The heart's concept, a steadfast way.

Through time and space, it holds its course,
A beacon bright, a driving force,
In every soul, its truth is kept,
The heart's concept, deeply wept.

Chromatic Reveries

In a sea of hues, my mind does swim,
Through valleys of blue, and peaks of crimson rim.
Golden whispers brush the silent skies,
A symphony of colors, where dreams arise.

Emerald fields stretch wide in the dawn,
Amber glows softly, where night has drawn.
Indigo shadows dance on walls unseen,
In these chromatic reveries, my soul is keen.

A palette of thoughts, each stroke a prayer,
Ochre warmth in the morning air.
Lavender light, draped over night's gown,
In hues and tints, all worries drown.

Turquoise ripples on the fabric of day,
Mirrored in violet, where shadows lay.
Scarlet whispers in the evening's breath,
In chromatic reveries, there's no death.

Narrative Whirlwind

In the tempest of tales, a wild spin,
Stories of old and new begin.
Whispers of legends, through time they trace,
In the narrative whirlwind, every face.

Words that dance, a ballet in the air,
Echoes of joy, of sorrow and care.
Verse upon verse, a cascading stream,
In this whirlwind, we weave our dream.

An epic saga, pages weathered and frail,
Heroes and villains, through time they sail.
Each chapter a storm, each line a breeze,
In the narrative whirlwind, hearts at ease.

A fable's end, a new one's start,
Bound by the rhythm, from heart to heart.
Stitches of stories, in tapestries blend,
In the whirlwind's eye, our souls mend.

Celestial Notions

Under the canopy of night's domain,
Stars whisper secrets, soft as rain.
Galaxies spin, in eternal flight,
In celestial notions, we find the light.

Moon whispers tales of lovers and kings,
Through lonely nights, its lullaby rings.
Planets in dance, a cosmic ballet,
In the notions of stars, we find our way.

Comets blaze trails in the velvet night,
Bright as our dreams, in their fleeting flight.
Nebulas cradle, in swirls of grace,
Celestial notions, our secret place.

Constellations trace, in patterns clear,
Stories of old, now drawing us near.
In the vast expanse, we dream and ponder,
In celestial notions, our souls wander.

Patterns in Chaos

Amid the tempest, in moments of despair,
Patterns emerge in the swirling air.
Chaos breathes life, in random disguise,
In its embrace, a beauty lies.

Fractals of thought, in tangled skein,
Order in chaos, the mind's refrain.
Waves of disorder, in currents shift,
Patterns in chaos, our spirits lift.

In tangled jungles, and star-streaked sky,
Symmetry dances, in chaos sly.
Hidden designs, in nature's spree,
In patterns of chaos, we feel free.

Randomness cloaks, what truth conveys,
In the chaos, meaning lays.
In life's upheaval, in tangled strife,
Patterns in chaos mirror our life.

Brushstrokes of Thought

In the quiet hum of twilight's sigh,
Colors swirl in patterns unknown,
Whispers blend where shadows lie,
On the canvas, dreams are sown.

Each stroke a dance of mind and hand,
Feelings pure, untold, serene,
Ideas take flight, so vast, so grand,
In the painter's silent scene.

Light and shade weave tender threads,
Mysteries born by moonlit streams,
Between reality and what is said,
Lie the painter's deepest dreams.

Soft hues cradle the fragile heart,
Reflections of a soul unveiled,
In each section, a story to impart,
By emotions, imagination sails.

Brushstrokes merge to form a whole,
Life depicted in silent waves,
Every piece, a part of the soul,
On art's vast sea, it bravely braves.

Ideas on a Breeze

Whispers drift on the winds of dawn,
Hints of thoughts yet to be known,
Glimpses of vistas far withdrawn,
Carried by breezes softly blown.

Seeds of wisdom on air's soft crest,
Inviting dreams to take their leap,
In the mind, they come to rest,
Awakening from slumber deep.

Ephemeral as a morning mist,
Yet, enduring in their grace,
Ideas in a gentle twist,
Transform the soul's embrace.

Inspiration rides the gale,
Echoes of a time to come,
Where ideas shimmer, never stale,
Their melody a gentle hum.

Caressed by whispers on the wing,
Thoughts unite in perfect form,
In the heart, they softly sing,
A symphony of dreams reborn.

Dreamscapes Unveiled

Through the veil of night's embrace,
Lies a realm where visions dwell,
Dreamscapes woven, soft in grace,
Where silent stories gently tell.

Stars ignite above the mind,
Paths unknown, brightly lit,
In dreams, pure truth we find,
Unseen threads the heart commits.

Wisps of shadow blend with light,
In this world, new worlds are made,
Unfolding secrets out of sight,
Where the heart's desires wade.

Each dream a chapter to explore,
In this vast and boundless sea,
Whispered wishes evermore,
Found in night's tranquility.

Dreamscapes vast, yet closely held,
Reveal the soul's deepest fare,
In these realms, the heart is spelled,
By the night, softly ensnared.

Vision's Hymn

In the heart's most sacred core,
Lies a vision, pure and bright,
Guiding paths we can't ignore,
Through the shadows, into light.

Each thought a note in life's grand song,
Harmonies of will and dream,
Visions weave where they belong,
In life's ever-flowing stream.

Eyes that see beyond the veil,
Piercing through the known facade,
Unveiling dreams that thus prevail,
In the soul, where visions prod.

With each step, the future sings,
Hymns of hope and boundless grace,
In the heart, a vision rings,
Guiding us through time and space.

The hymn of visions, clear and true,
Echoes in the silent mind,
Leading us to paths anew,
Where the soul and dreams entwine.

Mind's Canvas

Upon the canvas of the mind,
Where thoughts and dreams begin to bind,
Colors swirl in vivid hue,
Creating worlds both old and new.

Imagination takes its flight,
Through the day and through the night,
Every stroke a fresh idea,
Shaping visions far and near.

Whispers of a silent song,
Memories where they belong,
Painted with a gentle hand,
Moments like a grain of sand.

Mysteries in shadows play,
In the dark and light of day,
Concepts flow like rivers' streams,
In the gallery of dreams.

Patterns form and fade away,
Thoughts like clouds in skies of grey,
Yet in this mind's endless scene,
Every dream can find its sheen.

Waves of Inspiration

Waves of thought crash to the shore,
Ideas drift forevermore,
Inspiration's gentle rise,
Like the dawn meets morning skies.

Creativity's vast sea,
Endless as the mind can be,
Currents pull with unseen force,
Guiding us on new discourse.

Tide that brings the fresh and bold,
Stories yet to be retold,
Each crest brims with pure delight,
Echoes in the silent night.

Whirlpool of the wondrous mind,
Mysteries yet to unwind,
Fathoms deep of boundless thought,
Compass points where dreams are sought.

Sail upon this sea of muse,
Let no wind its light refuse,
Chart a course of endless grace,
Toward the horizon's embrace.

Epiphany in Silence

In silence lies a hidden truth,
Whispers of our fading youth,
Moments when the world stands still,
Ideas bloom of their own will.

Quiet is the fertile ground,
Where profound insights are found,
In the hush, a voice so clear,
Guides us to a vision dear.

Pause and let the silence speak,
Strength resides within the meek,
Epiphany in gentle shade,
Where the loudest thoughts are made.

Calm reveals what chaos hides,
In the stillness, wisdom bides,
Listen to the silent spark,
Lighting pathways in the dark.

To every noise, a counter sound,
In the quiet, thoughts abound,
Epiphanies like stars align,
In the silence, pure design.

Fires of Genius

In the heart, a flame ignites,
Burning with creative might,
Fires of genius fiercely blaze,
Casting light on shadowed ways.

Passion fuels the fervent mind,
Searing thoughts by fate entwined,
Every spark a burst of gold,
Wonders in the hand we hold.

Embers of a grand design,
Within the soul, visions shine,
Kindling dreams of future's gaze,
Through the fog of misty haze.

Ideas flare in fiery dance,
Chance and brilliance to enhance,
In the forge of intellect,
Dreams are built and thoughts reflect.

With each flame that breathes anew,
Worlds of wonder come to view,
Burning bright and ever high,
Fires of genius touch the sky.

Aspirations of the Soul

In the quiet dawn, dreams unfold,
Where whispers meet the morning light,
A tapestry of hopes untold,
A symphony of boundless flight.

Through valleys deep and mountains high,
The soul's journey, vast and grand,
With every star that lights the sky,
A beacon guiding heart and hand.

An endless quest for higher ground,
In each heartbeat, a fervent plea,
To seek, in silence, where truth's found,
And grasp the wings of destiny.

Resilience in each step we take,
A fragile thread, yet strong as steel,
In the soul's core, no storm can break,
A boundless strength that hearts reveal.

Through darkness, light, sorrow, and glee,
Aspirations of the soul rise,
To write our story, wild and free,
'Neath the canvas of endless skies.

Whispers of the Muse

In the hush of midnight's reign,
The muse whispers soft and clear,
Dreams take flight on thoughts unchained,
To realms of wonder, drawing near.

A world of shadows, light, and sound,
Where fantasies and truths entwine,
In every word, a vision found,
A spark to set the soul's design.

Through ink and pen, the muse imparts,
The echoes of a distant time,
In verses bound by humble hearts,
A melody, both sweet and prime.

Inspiration flows like gentle streams,
From whispered winds of ancient lore,
Awakening the deepest dreams,
And crafting tales forevermore.

So, heed the muse's quiet call,
Let imagination freely soar,
In endless nights where dreams enthrall,
Find the whispers you've waited for.

Kaleidoscope Hues

Beneath the arch of sky's embrace,
Colors blend in vibrant dance,
A spirit wild, devoid of trace,
In kaleidoscope hues' advance.

Each shade a voice, a tale to weave,
From amber dawn to twilight blue,
In every breath, the heart believes,
The world anew with every view.

Greens and golds of fields in bloom,
Crimson whispers in the dusk,
Within life's palette, joy and gloom,
Hues of dreams that never rust.

Melodies of rainbows bright,
In fractured light, a prism gleams,
Through every hue, a spark of light,
To paint the landscape of our dreams.

In this chromatic reverie,
The soul finds solace, colors true,
A world transformed by artistry,
In ever-changing kaleidoscope hues.

Lucid Dreamscapes

In realms where shadows softly creep,
Lucid dreamscapes come alive,
Whispers of a translucent deep,
In boundless spaces, we arrive.

Through veils of night, we softly tread,
On paths that shimmer, twist, and turn,
In the silent echoes, lightly spread,
Fires of wonder brightly burn.

A universe of endless flight,
Where gravity and time release,
In dreams, our visions reunite,
In waves of tranquil, flowing peace.

Each dreamscape, vivid, raw, and pure,
An atlas of the wandering mind,
In lucent layers, we endure,
A journey of a boundless kind.

We sail through stars, through night and day,
On wings of thought, through realms unseen,
In whispers of the dreams we sway,
With lucidity's gentle sheen.

Glimpse of Epiphany

In the quiet hush of dawn,
Where shadows softly creep,
A sudden truth is born,
From the silence deep.

Light breaks through the veil,
Of night's ephemeral lace,
Revealing paths once pale,
In a newfound space.

Epiphanies gently glow,
Within the heart's pure gaze,
Moments we come to know,
In life's enigmatic phase.

Boundless Horizons

Beyond the grasp of hand,
The sky unfolds its flight,
A realm where dreams expand,
And day transcends to night.

Mountains touch the sky,
With whispering winds so free,
Where endless visions lie,
In boundless ecstasy.

Oceans vast and deep,
Cradle stars beneath their waves,
In mystery they keep,
A tale that time engraves.

Clarity in Chaos

Amid the storm's embrace,
Where wild winds twist and turn,
A stillness finds its place,
In the heart we yearn.

Chaos knows no end,
Yet clarity does emerge,
In the wreckage, we mend,
From life's stormy surge.

Eyes open to the light,
In tempest's fervent strife,
Finding calm in the night,
A newfound lease on life.

The Dream Weaver

In the loom of night's domain,
A weaver works unseen,
Threading through joy and pain,
Crafting each dream's sheen.

Stars like silver thread,
Glimmer in cosmic loom,
Weaving tales in bed,
Beyond the cradle's room.

A tapestry of dreams,
Woven with care and love,
In moonlight's gentle beams,
From realms high above.

Whispers of Imagination

In corners of the mind's vast sea,
Where dreams cascade and wander free,
Soft whispers breathe, ignite the spark,
Illuminating realms of dark.

A flicker here, a shadow there,
Ideas rise from thought's soft flare,
Forming worlds untouched by hand,
In this vast, ethereal land.

Silent songs of untamed grace,
Reveal themselves in subtle trace,
Sketching tales in shades unseen,
In the mind's enchanting scene.

Yet fleeting, like the morning mist,
These visions dance, then cease, desist,
Leaving whispers, faint, yet bold,
In realms where imaginations unfold.

The Canvas of Minds

Upon the canvas, blank and wide,
Our thoughts and dreams in worlds collide,
A brushstroke here, a color bright,
Creating realms of boundless light.

Each hue a memory, clear or vague,
Painting stories that never fade,
In shades of hope and shadows cast,
A tapestry of futures past.

With every line, a story told,
Mysteries in pigments bold,
Capturing the essence true,
Of minds that dream in every hue.

The canvas grows with each new thought,
A masterpiece, by time, unsought,
Reflecting journeys deep inside,
The swirling depths where visions bide.

Echoes in Abstract

In realms where form and function blur,
Ideas abstract softly stir,
Echoes from the mind's deep well,
Resonating, casting spell.

Shapes that twist in phantom flight,
Contours lost in shadowed light,
Boundless, endless, undefined,
Such are echoes in the mind.

Patterns shift and weave anew,
Creating paths both old and true,
In the abstract, truths reside,
Whispered on the mental tide.

Elusive whispers, abstract thought,
Meaning found in lines we've sought,
An endless dance of form and sound,
In swirling echoes, we are found.

Light Through Shadows

In shadows deep where secrets lie,
A glimmer bright will catch the eye,
Piercing through the darkened veil,
A story told where lights prevail.

Soft rays that dance on edges sharp,
Illuminating hidden arcs,
Breaking through the sable night,
Revealing whispered truths in light.

Each shadow holds a hidden grace,
Light weaves patterns, forms a space,
Showing paths where hope resides,
Guided by the light's soft tides.

Through darkness thick, a journey sought,
Light and shadow, battles fought,
Until at last, the dawn reveals,
The beauty light through shadow seals.

The Art of Seeing

In shadows cast by twilight's hand,
A stillness wraps the sleeping land,
Through veils of dusk, the secrets peep,
In quiet mists, the echoes seep.

Eyes embrace the hidden light,
In gentle whispers of the night,
Each silhouette a tale to tell,
In every leaf where dreams compel.

Colors blend in hues unseen,
A canvas painted serene,
Nature's brush strokes soft and slow,
In glimmers faint we seek to know.

Patterns form in silent dance,
Underneath the moon's soft trance,
Revealed are truths, so subtle, grand,
In the art of seeing's gentle hand.

Where vision meets the inner gaze,
A world anew in soft displays,
Unseen by those who merely look,
But found by those who read the book.

Fragments of Genius

In shards of thoughts that flicker free,
A brilliance glimpsed in reverie,
Ideas dance on edge of night,
In fragments forming beams of light.

Scattered dreams in mind's expanse,
Converge to form a fleeting glance,
Of inspirations' whispered tune,
Beneath the sky, above the dune.

Eureka sparks, a burning flame,
Within the chaos, finds its name,
In broken bits a mosaic lies,
A masterpiece beneath the skies.

Through prisms of the fractured soul,
A genius manifests its whole,
Capturing the essence rare,
In fragments scattered everywhere.

In chaos born of boundless seas,
Brilliance shines in mysteries,
For in the scattered light we find,
The genius of a restless mind.

Epiphanies in Bloom

Beneath the dawn, where whispers weave,
An epiphany takes its leave,
From petals soft, a secret borne,
In morning light, a soul reborn.

Silent thoughts like flowers bloom,
In gardens of a twilight's gloom,
Each revelation gently sways,
In unseen winds of bygone days.

The mind unfurls in soft array,
As insights rise with break of day,
In revelations' tender glow,
The seeds of wisdom start to grow.

Amongst the blossoms, shadows play,
In hidden nooks where light might stray,
Each bloom a tale of sudden sight,
Epiphanies in morning light.

As petals part, the truth reveals,
In nature's calm, the spirit heals,
Through every bloom, a mindful grace,
A timeless story, face to face.

A Symphony of Notions

In tumbling waves of thoughts that breeze,
A symphony amidst the trees,
Notions play in harmony grand,
Conducted by an unseen hand.

Each thought a note in mind's expanse,
Together form a mystic dance,
With every whisper, every sigh,
A symphony beneath the sky.

Ideas rise in crescendos bright,
Under the canopy of night,
In every star a verse is sown,
In constellations thought has grown.

Melodies of musings drift,
In currents strong, in tempests swift,
An orchestra of dreams unbound,
In soulful waves of thought profound.

Where silence reigns, the music swells,
In quiet minds where wisdom dwells,
A symphony of notions plays,
Through nights and into dawning days.

Milton Keynes UK
Ingram Content Group UK Ltd.
UKHW020004010824
446405UK00003B/38

9 789916 863190